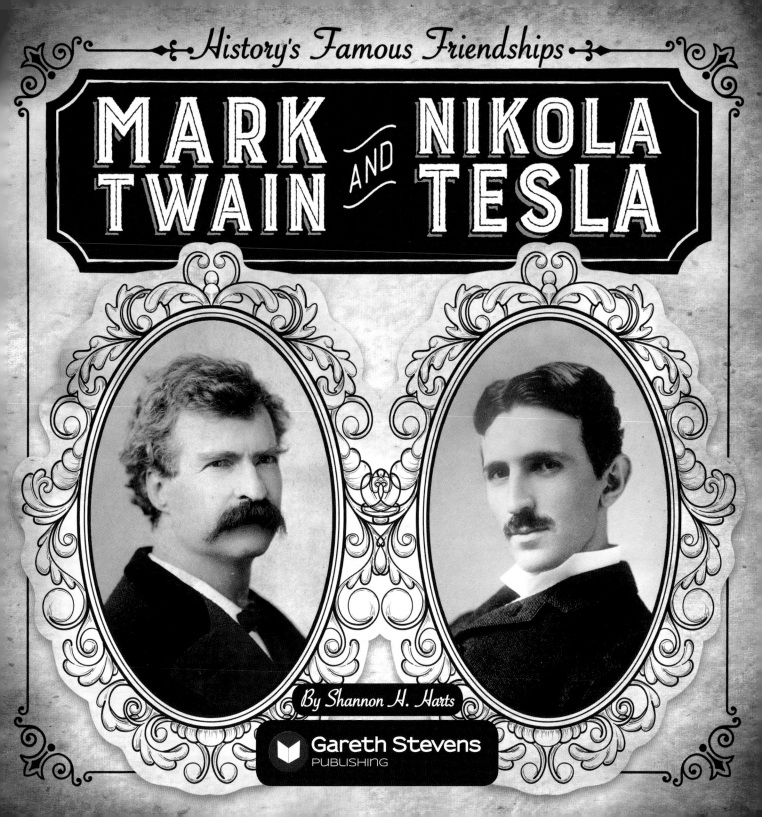

History's Famous Friendships

MARK TWAIN AND NIKOLA TESLA

By Shannon H. Harts

Gareth Stevens
PUBLISHING

Please visit our website, www.garethstevens.com. For a free color catalog of all our high-quality books, call toll free 1-800-542-2595 or fax 1-877-542-2596.

Library of Congress Cataloging-in-Publication Data

Names: Harts, Shannon H., author.
Title: Mark Twain and Nikola Tesla / Shannon H. Harts.
Description: New York : Gareth Stevens Publishing, [2022] | Series:
   History's famous friendships | Includes index.
Identifiers: LCCN 2020036359 (print) | LCCN 2020036360 (ebook) | ISBN
   9781538265031 (library binding) | ISBN 9781538265017 (paperback) | ISBN
   9781538265024 (set) | ISBN 9781538265048 (ebook)
Subjects: LCSH: Twain, Mark, 1835-1910--Friends and associates--Juvenile
   literature. | Tesla, Nikola, 1856-1943--Friends and associates--Juvenile
   literature. | Authors, American--19th century--Biography--Juvenile
   literature. | Inventors--United States--19th
   century--Biography--Juvenile literature. | Male friendship--United
   States--History--Juvenile literature.
Classification: LCC PS1333 .H37 2022 (print) | LCC PS1333 (ebook) | DDC
   621.3092 [B]--dc23
LC record available at https://lccn.loc.gov/2020036359
LC ebook record available at https://lccn.loc.gov/2020036360

First Edition

Published in 2022 by
Gareth Stevens Publishing
111 East 14th Street, Suite 349
New York, NY 10003

Copyright © 2022 Gareth Stevens Publishing

Designer: Katelyn E. Reynolds
Editor: Therese Shea

Photo credits: Cvr, pp. 1 (Twain), 7, 27 Library of Congress/Corbis/VCG via Getty Images; cvr, p. 1 (Tesla), 9 (Tesla) Napoleon Sarony/Fine Art Images/Heritage Images/Getty Images; cvr, pp. 1-32 (background) wawritto/Shutterstock.com; pp. 1-32 (frame) Olesia Misty/Shutterstock.com; cvr, pp. 1-32 (border) Vasya Kobelev/Shutterstock.com; p. 5 Kostich/FPG/Archive Photos/ Getty Images; p. 5 (Tesla) Jacques Boyer/Roger Viollet via Getty Images; p. 9 Underwood Archives/Getty Images; p. 9 (Edison), 14, 15, 29 Bettmann/Getty Images; p. 11 John Parrot/Stocktrek Images/Getty Images; p. 13 (inset) Originally published as part of an article by T.C. Martin called "Tesla's Oscillator and Other Inventions" that appeared in the Century Magazine (April 1895)/PRODUCER/Wikipedia.org; p. 13 Albert Harlingue/Roger Viollet via Getty Images; pp. 16, 24 Culture Club/ Getty Images; p. 17 Fine Art Images/Heritage Images/Getty Images; p. 19 (inset) Retrieved from http://www.museumsyndicate. com/item.php?item=49426./Wdwd/Wikipedia.org; p. 19 Stefano Bianchetti/Corbis via Getty Images; p. 21 (inset) http:// www.teslauniverse.com/nikola-tesla-timeline-1895-tesla-looses-fifth-ave-lab-to-fire/My-wikiphotos/Wikipedia. org; p. 21 PhotoQuest/Getty Images; p. 23 (inset) Nikola Tesla Museum, Belgrad/Свифт/Wikipedia.org; p. 23 ullstein bild/ ullstein bild via Getty Images; p. 25 (inset) Kypros/Moment/Getty Images; p. 25 Originally published in "Tesla's Important Advances" in Electrical Review, May 20, 1896, p. 263. Credited in caption to Tonnelé and Co./Scewing/Wikipedia.org; p. 27 (inset) Beinecke Rare Book and Manuscript Library [1] (http://beinecke.library.yale.edu/dl_crosscollex/brbldl_getrec. asp?fld=img&id=1065313)/Soerfm/Wikipedia.org; p. 28 SolomonCrowe/iStock Unreleased/Getty Images; p. 29 (Twain) Hulton Archive/Getty Images.

Printed in the United States of America

CPSIA compliance information: Batch #CSGS22: For further information contact Gareth Stevens, New York, New York at 1-800-542-2595.

Find us on

CONTENTS

Words in the Glossary appear in **bold** type the first time they are used in the text.

TWO TALENTS

The **Industrial Revolution** of the 1700s and 1800s brought great changes in **technology** and society to many parts of the world. By the end of the 1800s, scientists had discovered a lot about electricity and how to use it.

Inventor Nikola Tesla and author Samuel Clemens (better known by the **pen name** Mark Twain) became friends during this time. Tesla and Twain were from different countries and did different kinds of work. However, their interest in science brought them together.

MORE TO KNOW

SOME CALL THE LATE 1800s AND EARLY 1900s, DURING WHICH TESLA AND TWAIN LIVED, THE SECOND INDUSTRIAL REVOLUTION. SCIENTISTS THEN LEARNED MUCH ABOUT ELECTRICITY, STEEL, FUELS, AND PLASTICS.

4

Mark Twain

Twain visited the lab where Tesla worked several times. Twain once wrote in a letter to his sister, "An inventor is a poet——a true poet."

Nikola Tesla

5

THE AUTHOR'S EARLY LIFE

Mark Twain was born Samuel Clemens on November 30, 1835, in Florida, Missouri. In 1839, his family moved to the nearby town of Hannibal. When he was 11, his father died. He soon became an **apprentice** at the *Missouri Courier* newspaper. He helped support his family.

Clemens's older brother Orion bought a newspaper in 1851. Clemens wrote and made drawings for the paper. Before long, readers could see his sense of humor in his work. He later wrote more than 20 books as Mark Twain.

MORE TO KNOW

IN HIS EARLY 20s, SAMUEL CLEMENS BECAME A RIVERBOAT PILOT, OR SOMEONE WHO STEERS RIVERBOATS. HIS PEN NAME, MARK TWAIN, CAME FROM A RIVERBOAT TERM THAT MEANS 12 FEET (3.6 M) DEEP.

Twain in front of his boyhood home

Hannibal, Missouri, is on the Mississippi River. Twain's books *The Adventures of Tom Sawyer* and *The Adventures of Huckleberry Finn* took place in a town much like it.

THE INVENTOR'S EARLY LIFE

On July 10, 1856, Nikola Tesla was born in what is now Croatia. As a child, he had a strong imagination. Tesla studied **engineering** in school. When he was in his 20s, he planned how to use **alternating current (AC)** to power motors and lights.

In 1882, Tesla started working for the Continental Edison electric company in Paris, France. He sailed to New York City in 1884 to work directly with inventor Thomas Edison. Edison wasn't interested in Tesla's ideas about AC, though. Tesla soon quit.

MORE TO KNOW

EDISON BELIEVED **DIRECT CURRENT (DC)** WAS THE BEST KIND OF ELECTRICAL CURRENT. TESLA LATER WORKED FOR GEORGE WESTINGHOUSE, WHO BELIEVED AC WAS BETTER. A "WAR OF THE CURRENTS" BEGAN. (AC BECAME THE MORE COMMON POWER SOURCE.)

Tesla said that when he heard about Niagara Falls as a child, he imagined "a big wheel run by the falls." As an adult, he helped create machinery that uses Niagara Falls to produce electricity.

Thomas Edison

Nikola Tesla

9

A NEW FRIENDSHIP IN NEW YORK

Twain and Tesla's friendship began in the 1890s. Twain had **invested** in electric motors in the 1880s. He later heard about an AC electric motor that Tesla had invented for George Westinghouse's company. But Twain was also thinking about investing in a DC motor invented by James W. Paige.

Tesla warned Twain not to invest in the DC motor, and Twain didn't. Twain recognized that Tesla's motor was the better product. Twain and Tesla's shared interest in technology led to a friendship.

MORE TO KNOW

IN THE 1870s, TESLA WAS SO SICK HE ALMOST DIED. HE READ MANY OF TWAIN'S STORIES DURING THIS TIME. HE SAID THEY WERE SO INTERESTING THEY MADE HIM "FORGET MY HOPELESS STATE."

Tesla built a machine called a magnifying transmitter in his New York City lab. It could make huge sparks of electricity.

A LAB OF WONDERS

Tesla and Twain had a deep interest in each other's work. Tesla trusted Twain to see his inventions. In 1894, he invited Twain to his New York City lab on South Fifth Avenue, which is today's West Broadway.

Twain and a few of Tesla's other friends took part in experiments. They also saw amazing machines Tesla had built, such as the Tesla coil. A Tesla coil uses a changing magnetic field to produce lightning-like flashes of electricity that can be many feet long.

MORE TO KNOW

THE TESLA COIL WAS THE FIRST INVENTION THAT COULD SEND ELECTRICITY WITHOUT ANY WIRES.

Tesla coil

At left, Twain is holding one of Tesla's inventions, a **vacuum** lamp, which got its power from a Tesla coil.

PART OF THE EXPERIMENT

During one visit to the lab, Tesla showed Twain a machine called an electromechanical oscillator. It was also called an "earthquake machine" because it created vibrations, or shaking movements, like an earthquake does. Tesla thought of another interesting use for it, though.

Tesla knew Twain had **digestion** problems. He suggested Twain stand on the vibrating plate of the machine. Twain agreed, and the earthquake machine soon helped his digestion trouble!

Mark Twain

While Tesla created around 300 inventions,
he's most known for making modern electricity possible.

A CLUB'S KINDNESS

In 1888, Twain helped found a club in New York City called The Players where actors could meet people in other fields, such as music, writing, and business. Twain invited Tesla to be a member in 1894. It became a place Tesla could be found when he wasn't in his lab.

On March 13, 1895, a fire broke out at Tesla's lab. He lost nearly everything. To cheer him up, The Players put on a concert just for him.

Mark Twain.

After the fire at his lab, Tesla told a newspaper that he was "in too much grief [sadness] to talk." He had lost inventions, notes, tools, photos, and more.

A NEW START

The fire was a major blow to Tesla's career. He had lost most of his inventions in the flames. However, he didn't give up on his dreams. Friends helped him raise money. He rented a new lab in July 1895. It was on East Houston Street in New York City.

Tesla decided to take his inventing ideas in different directions. In addition to wireless electricity, he studied **radio waves.** Also, an experiment with Twain nearly led to Tesla discovering X-rays.

MORE TO KNOW

X-RAYS ARE A POWERFUL TYPE OF ENERGY THAT CANNOT BE SEEN BY THE HUMAN EYE. THEY CAN TRAVEL THROUGH SKIN AND SOME OTHER SOLID SURFACES.

In 1899, Tesla built another lab (shown above and at left) in Colorado Springs, Colorado.

19

A SURPRISING PHOTO

Around 1895, while Twain was in Tesla's New York lab, the men performed an experiment with a vacuum tube. Tesla wanted to use the vacuum tube and a Tesla coil to take a picture of Twain. At first, Tesla thought the picture hadn't worked at all. It showed a shadowy image of a screw in the camera lens.

Later, Tesla learned German scientist Wilhelm Röntgen had discovered X-rays. Tesla then understood that his vacuum tube had produced an X-ray image of the camera screw.

MORE TO KNOW

TESLA'S PICTURE OF THE CAMERA SCREW MAY HAVE BEEN THE FIRST X-RAY IMAGE TAKEN IN THE UNITED STATES. TWAIN AND TESLA LATER TOOK TURNS USING TESLA'S "X-RAY GUN" TO TAKE PICTURES OF EACH OTHER'S BODIES!

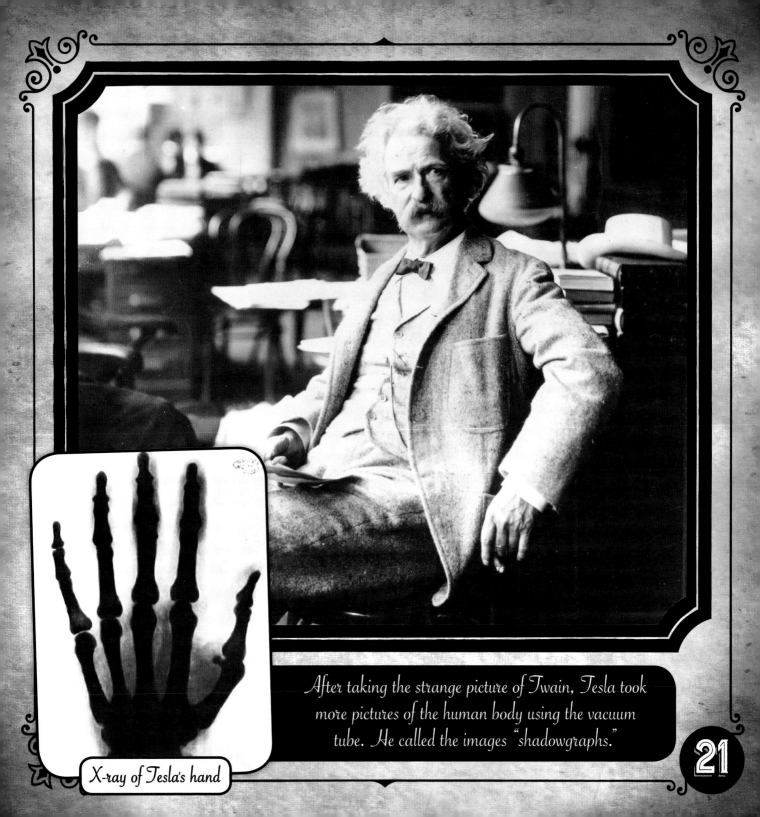

X-ray of Tesla's hand

After taking the strange picture of Twain, Tesla took more pictures of the human body using the vacuum tube. He called the images "shadowgraphs."

A NEW KIND OF WARSHIP

The Spanish-American War took place in 1898. That year, Tesla got a patent for an invention that he thought could be used in other wars. This machine was a small boat controlled by radio waves. It didn't need a driver or any other person on it. Tesla believed such boats could take the place of battleships and save soldiers' lives.

Tesla offered the patent to the U.S. Army. However, the army turned him down. Twain, who was in Europe, found out about Tesla's radio-controlled ship.

MORE TO KNOW

A PATENT IS AN OFFICIAL PAPER THAT GIVES AN INVENTOR THE RIGHTS TO A PLAN, MACHINE, OR PROCESS FOR A TIME. IT GUARDS THEIR WORK SO OTHERS CAN'T STEAL THEIR IDEAS.

Tesla's boat

Tesla showed people how his boat worked at the 1898 Electrical Exhibition. An exhibition is an event at which people can see objects of interest.

A DRONE BEFORE ITS TIME

In a letter to Tesla, Twain asked if Tesla would allow him to sell patents in Europe for the radio-controlled boat. Twain said he had been talking with others about how nations could be forced to stop using **weapons** and waging war. Twain had told people that they should "invite the great inventors" to come up with "something against which fleets and armies would be helpless." Twain wrote that he was surprised Tesla had already invented such a machine.

modern drone

Tesla's exact machine didn't make it into the military. However, the radio-wave technology it used led to the invention of today's drones. Drones are a kind of aircraft that can fly without a pilot on board.

25

A TIME-TRAVELING ENGINEER

Twain's interest in science **inspired** some of his writing. It's possible Tesla's work inspired him too. In 1889, Twain's book *A Connecticut Yankee in King Arthur's Court* came out. It was about an engineer who travels back in time from the 1800s to the 500s.

The engineer, Hank Morgan, tries to share what he knows from the 19th century to improve people's lives in the sixth century. However, some people fight his efforts, and he has to use his inventions to work against them.

MORE TO KNOW

TESLA'S WORK MAY HAVE INSPIRED A SHORT STORY TWAIN WROTE IN 1898 ABOUT A MACHINE CALLED A TELECTROSCOPE. IT CREATED SOMETHING A BIT LIKE TODAY'S INTERNET!

Some early copies of Twain's time-travel book had different titles. Twain is shown at his desk in 1901.

INSPIRING FRIENDS

Mark Twain died on April 21, 1910, at age 74. Tesla died on January 7, 1943, at age 86. Both men had changed the world through their work.

Tesla's ideas about AC brought about the modern electrical systems that provide power to our communities. Twain's books still entertain and inspire readers and authors. In fact, many young people read and study them in school. These men worked in different fields, but they shared an excitement about what technology could do in the future.

Tesla statue in Niagara Falls

A Timeline of Two Friends

1835
Samuel Clemens is born on November 30 in Florida, Missouri.

1856
Nikola Tesla is born in Croatia on July 10.

1870s
Twain's books comfort Tesla during an illness.

1880s
Twain speaks with Tesla about electric motors.

1889
A Connecticut Yankee in King Arthur's Court is released, inspired by Twain's interest in science.

1894
Twain invites Tesla to join the club The Players.

1895
Twain helps Tesla produce what's likely the first X-ray image taken in the United States.

1898
Twain writes to Tesla about his radio-controlled boat.

1909
Twain invites Tesla to his daughter's wedding.

1910
Twain dies on April 21.

1943
Tesla dies on January 7.

GLOSSARY

alternating current (AC): an electric current that reverses, or switches its direction, often and regularly

apprentice: someone who learns a trade by working with a skilled person of that trade

digestion: the breakdown of food inside the body so that the body can use it

direct current (DC): an electric current that flows in only one direction

engineering: the use of science and math to build better objects

Industrial Revolution: an era of social and economic changes marked by advances in technology and science

inspire: to cause someone to want to do something

invest: to spend money on a project in order to make more money in the future

pen name: a name used when writing instead of a real name

radio waves: a pattern of electrical and magnetic fields that can be used to send signals through the air without wires

technology: the way people do something using tools and the tools that they use

vacuum: a space in which nearly all gas has been removed

weapon: something used to cause someone or something injury or death

For More Information

Books

Fankhouser, Kris. *How I Changed the World: Nikola Tesla.* Chicago, IL: World Book, Inc., 2018

Hermann, Spring. *Reading and Interpreting the Works of Mark Twain.* New York, NY: Enslow Publishing, 2018.

Twain, Mark. *The Adventures of Tom Sawyer.* San Diego, CA: Printers Row Publishing Group, 2019.

Websites

Biography: Mark Twain
www.ducksters.com/biography/authors/mark_twain.php
Read about Mark Twain's life and work.

Edison vs. Tesla
www.energy.gov/edison-vs-tesla
Find out more about Tesla, Edison, and the War of the Currents.

Who Was Nikola Tesla?
www.wonderopolis.org/wonder/who-was-nikola-tesla
Learn more about Tesla's world-changing inventions.

INDEX